Along the Forest Corridor

Also by Paul Williamson and published by Ginninderra Press
Edge of Southern Bright
A Hint of Eden

Paul Williamson

Along the Forest Corridor

Acknowledgements

Poems in this volume have been published in
Quadrant, Milestones, Landcare Annual Report,
Redhill Regenerators website, *Polestar, Positive Words* and *Tamba*.

Thanks to family and friends for support and the shared experiences from which I drew.
Thanks are due to Michael Mulvaney for expert nature advice and to Les Wicks for a poetry edit.

Along the Forest Corridor
ISBN 978 1 76109 589 4
Copyright © text Paul Williamson 2023
Cover image by the author – Yellow Box, Red Hill, ACT

First published 2023 by
GINNINDERRA PRESS
PO Box 3461 Port Adelaide 5015
www.ginninderrapress.com.au

Contents

Nature Haven
- Scouting — 11
- Nature Corridor — 12
- Seasonal Rush — 13
- Breeding Time Eyes — 14
- Surge of Spring — 15
- Bouncing Back — 16
- Numbers — 18
- As it Warmed — 20
- The Long Dry — 21
- Summer Smoke — 22
- Black Summer all around — 23
- Storms — 24
- Sunday Scuttle — 25
- Disappearing Wetlands — 26
- Joy smiles on the strangeness — 27
- A Flutter of Hope — 28
- Still more birds come back — 29
- What Grows Back — 30
- Looking Forward Looking Back — 31
- Journeys of the Young — 32
- Changing Times — 34

Other Residents
- The Move — 37
- Echidna — 38
- Welcome Back — 39
- Tree of Life — 40
- Sentinels — 41
- The Gang — 42

Private Party	43
Resurrections	44
There Are Dragons	45
Cunningham Skink	46
To the Zone	47
Meeting a Local	48
The Fledgling	49
Sodden	50
Cool Time	51
Patches	52
Echoes in the Night	53
Remnants	54
Teaching	55
Juliet Who Survived the Fox	56
On a Branch	57
Saving the Future	58
She Oak Bloom	59
Winter Welcome	60

Visitors

Yellow-tailed Black Cockatoos	63
The Return	64
After Dry Years	65
Rarely	66
Rain Chasers	67
Among the Leaves	68
Returning to the Hollow	69
Robins	71
On the Move	72
From the Storm	73
Long Distance Little Eagle	74
Painted Ladies	76

Pasture Day Moth	77
Something New	78
Wood Ducks	79
Scarce	80
Leaving the Nest	81
Family Feud	82
Skirmish	83

Forest Grounding

The Climb	87
Naming Seasons	88
A Different Path	89
Along the Track	90
Two years after Black Summer	91
Recharge	92
Listening	93

Nature Haven

Scouting

Trudging upwards towards a full egg-yellow moon
I turn and crunch the ridge to the top of the hill.
Magpies swoop and squabble over territory;
bats flitter from among ancient trees, snatching insects
from the open sky; sparse eastern grey kangaroos
graze by the trail. The light show in the balmy

dusk is from factories near the airport;
guide lights for one plane landing, another circling;
parliament's stare and along the valleys
the glows of Weston, Gungahlin and Tuggeranong; changes
of traffic lights, amber street lamps flickering
and steady white security boundaries.
I reach a sense of knowing what I see.

Warriors climbed this ridge under Ngunnawal skies
to scan below for hunting smoke and campfires
lit by groups that migrated from one food source
to the next; from kangaroo to bogong moth.
Now the smoke is from burn-back to curb bushfires.
What I scan is not from trails of tribal groups
but for the thousands heading for city meals.

Nature Corridor

This is the longest forest haven
in eastern Australia; straggling from the surfing coast
across the misty escarpment
to our more level country near Canberra.
Here tracks are winding lanes
that shuffle over friendly Red Hill Reserve

where yellow box eucalypts live for hundreds of years;
parrots and possums nest in their hollows.
Vistas change like rooms in gardens
and charm with rocky gullies.
Ribbons of she oaks and sculptured gum trees
shelter rainbows of small birds, and statuesque kangaroos.

Away from well-trodden tracks
trees crowd and scrub looms
tangled tea tree branches protect.

Seasonal Rush

Spring deceives and chases;
the swooping magpie, a male
stark black and white, furiously
speeds the ducking cyclist
from near the five-tree hill.

Kookaburras laugh but they are serious.
The pair high on the wire warns in chorus
another heading across their claimed ground.
One breaks, flying straight and hard
to make sure the intruder leaves.

The red wattlebird rasps a ritual warning
then harries a crow away from the grevilleas;
forgetting size, spurred by fury.
The hen is hidden in the crush of leaf and flower.
I am still not sure of all that the anger protects.

Breeding Time Eyes

The buck kangaroo joins the group
of does that stand alert; he lazes
in end of winter sun; a joey
leans from a pouch to nibble grass.

Reaping with maternal fervour
a spotted pardalote, stark white spots
but without the bright red of the male
flits from leaf to leaf along a giving branch.

A troupe of currawongs spreads through the trees
calling back and forth about prey;
probes the leaf litter searching
away from their diet of berries.

Glistening ravens with shaggy necks
stare from high perches
moan about impending deaths
in their search for flesh to fill their eggs.

Surge of Spring

In dawns of new birth
trees are quiet
while in hidden nests and hollows
hens warm eggs;
cock birds bring food.

Six weeks later noise is back
from big-eyed rosellas fledglings
rich coloured with black-lined backs
flying and squabbling in small groups.
Dim-hued magpie young squawk
at harried parents to be fed.

A crèche of black-faced cuckoo shrikes
chases single file from high tree to high tree
kestrel fledglings watch from their branch.

Blossoms burst out in warmer light.
Insects and caterpillars fatten
on leaves and lush grass.
Kangaroos graze and spar
as nature climbs another step.

Bouncing Back

Two months of savage summer heat
leaves struggling plants dotting the reserve
while the young wedge-tailed eagle strengthens
on the deaths of eastern grey wallabies.

Showers roll from the west;
steady drenching rain ends the dire spell.
Kangaroos lounge on lush grass
a hop away from more growth by the fire trail.

The kestrel family returns
to check their nest site;
the youngster gliding with good shape.
A noisy friarbird and a grey butcherbird
snatch insects from moist air.

Grey fantails flurry in a swollen mixed flock.
Thornbills with yellow flashes
hop and light up the grass. Among the leaves
small grey-green shapes flit;
there may be weebills, unidentified.

A pair of scarlet robins makes an entrance;
as half hidden among the autumn greenery
a speckled warbler perches still and silent
masked grey face; flecked breast
buff-striped wings.

Currawongs scour the treetops
but don't see the smaller birds
hidden among the mixed flock;
as the brutal hot spell is forgotten.

Numbers

Kangaroos spread on the rocky hill
grazing recent rain
looking like rounded boulders.
They raise their heads to watch us climb
pouches hung heavy with joeys
avoiding the early spring chill.
But numbers have grown
to four figures from the latest yearly count
still they seem healthy, thick-coated and relaxed
grazing the slope.
Grass is cropped to a few centimetres
as regular as a sheep paddock;
autumn rain and warm weather has spurred growth
to thirty centimetres under the blackthorn tangle.
But the question slowly starts to worry.
What will feed this season's young
through the hard winter?

The big buck kangaroo is back
to graze the winter grass in the front yard
where fronts of rain have made it lush.
He comes from the reserve where grass is short;
standing man tall – worth a wary eye.

I pass four metres from him on my way
to the letter box. He stays crouched
hands on the ground like a sprinter
on starting blocks, powerful – in good condition.
He hardly interrupts his lunch to look
as I go back to the house. He doesn't bother me.

On the hill kangaroos search beside the hard-baked track
among the dirt and dead leaves
to feed on last stems of straw.
Through the night small groups
of does and joeys jump fences
to bound along roads like they own the hill.
Our grey brown lawn is kangaroo mowed
morning droppings scattered.
A joey stands at the street corner
alone and looking away.

As it Warmed

The months of heatwave drag into March
breaking the record for the hottest summer.
On the hill grass is dusty dead.

A eucalypt centenarian ringed with dry leaves
has steel grey stripes on the yellow-buff trunk
that had spread thick limbs in its glory.
Some are broken now or dying back.

On the shaded lower slope
young offspring suffer less.
The youngest even seem to thrive
with scribble bark tattoos.

The high tree looks to be air-baked, drifting
into dreaming afterlife
to set more homes for nature.

The Long Dry

Our forest view is into distance
like when indigenous hunters cleared with cold fires.
Leaves have died
and lie on baked dirt.
Curled bark splits and sheds
leaving iron-stained and sallow-camouflage trunks.

On the hillside grass has gone
but kangaroos slowly search for shoots.
Button daisies struggle to hold blooms.
Birds are slow and sparse. Crimson rosellas
feed in house gardens near the reserve.
This sapping decade dictates
we don't water thin lawns
where night kangaroos leave droppings.

Remnant forest scrub survives in shade
as centurion giants tap fissures in the granite hill
but most eucalypts sacrifice branches.
Two tall trees die to grey in weeks
lasting tombstones from this long dry.

Summer Smoke

The mounting wind flares coals
towards threat where local burns
still smoulder.

A grey fantail swirls unconcerned
and perches two metres from the track.
Close by eastern grey kangaroos graze.

A pair of wedge-tailed eagles drifts
from Mugga Ridge to above our hill
to hunt in easy circles.

The rescue helicopter pulses to the hospital.

Black Summer all around

killed thirty-three by fire, four hundred and forty by smoke
after record-breaking drought.
Thousands went to hospital.
More than three thousand homes were lost.
Twenty million hectares burned.
Three billion wildlife were killed; kangaroos, koalas, reptiles, birds.
We pray they restock through good seasons.

For three months we breathed smoke.
often not seeing past a hundred metres.
People watched fires from beach sands.
City buildings circulated bad air;
almost nowhere to escape it
even behind filter masks.
Businesses took hits and struggle to rebuild.
For many a step towards their end
veins, hearts and minds.

Storms

The day is ashen and heavy.
Branches barely move.

Walking to beat the twilight
as lighting flashes
and distant thunder rumbles, we turn

on the rocky hillside to watch
a wall of soot-coloured, ribbed, threatening
thunderhead rearing skyward.

A silver streak targets the hilltop trig.
The voice is thunder;
Lightning.

Hard rain falls.

Sunday Scuttle

Rain pocks the lake
fed by muddy flows from creeks.
Ducks fossick regardless.

Puddles on paths force tracks
that skirt the edges
as walkers search for cover

then huddle under leaking eucalypts
to worry about distant thunder.
Thornbills pipe distractedly in the scrub

while drops slide, tease dry seeds to grow.

Disappearing Wetlands

Steady rain has refilled Canberra lakes
and catchments after the long dry
so the Jerrabomberra Wetlands is due
a flush of birdlife.
But the wetlands have gone;
only a grassy paddock in a shallow valley remains.
A small mixed flock flits along the bushy edge;
a grey fantail, fire tailed finches and a New England honeyeater.

Water birds don't paddle where the lake used to be
no Australasian black ducks or pink-eared ducks
with their zebra stripes, no grebes to surface and disappear.
Empty hides show hopeful photos
of birds that once lived or visited here.

A cyclist muses past staring at this birdwatcher.
The enclosed and reengineered sewerage treatment plant
across the road has ponds with some swamp hens.
The creek near the former wetlands
is fuller than ever down to surging waterside apartments
but life in the wetlands is sparse.

Joy smiles on the strangeness

of the wetlands at last growing lush
after a decade of drought
then months of rain.
Small birds, drought survivors
are back at last but flit nervously
and are barely glimpsed;
reed warblers, cisticolas, honeyeaters.

Scrub wrens have remained
to navigate the undergrowth
as troupes of blue wrens twitter.
Red-rumped parrots, lethargic
snooze in tall casuarinas
while their young in muted blue
feed on the seed heads on tall grasses.

Water birds spread across the lake;
pelicans, black ducks with ducklings
moor hens, grebes and coot.
Frogs croak and drum in muddy lows
where thirsty earth has not sponged the water.

In the Black Mountain gardens, protected
by government from the worst of the dry
birds are more relaxed.
New England honeyeaters and eastern spinebills
seem to barely notice watchers.
Crimson honeyeaters have come this year
from burned-out eastern forests.

A Flutter of Hope

It has been ten years since I saw
a mixed flock of small birds.
Today a flock swirls and flits in the trees;
a white-eared honeyeater from the hills
migrating from late winter chill;
grey fantails with their flourish;
thorn bills, a group of tiny stubby weebills.

I note them down in my bird book
check the last date and know
it was before the drought
and Black Summer that burned out forests
to the close-by Brindabellas.
Growth returned after last year's rain
now the small birds with their flashes of hope.

Still more birds come back

by mid-spring to secluded thicker forest.
Noisy friarbirds former heralds of the season
feed among leafy tops of gum tree saplings
quiet in nesting time.

At the hill top, high in a eucalypt
two black-faced cuckoo shrikes are shadowed
by currawongs likely near their nest.
They seem to be passing through
as they return to dipping flight.

What Grows Back

Bare, dusty dry
before the rains at last came
the hill is lush green again.
The kangaroos no longer dine out
on neighbourhood lawns and verges.
Trees seem sturdier.

Eastern slopes glow purple
with Paterson's Curse
blooming poison for horses.
Blackberry bushes surge
in spite of yearly spraying.
Thistle patches rise rampant
winking colour.

Through twenty-five steadfast years
after sheep and cattle stopped grazing
the nature group has cut back weeds
from three to one-quarter cover.
They might have believed
that with nature at their back
their work was almost done
but the hill calls them again.

Looking Forward Looking Back

Plastic sleeves green the ridge now
guarding seedlings of plants that grew here
when settlers came;
yellow box eucalypts, she oak and wattle.

Groves from last year's plantings stand apart
within the walls of felled invasive plants
placed to keep kangaroos at bay.
Sheep and cattle no longer graze

as volunteers work to reforest.
Kangaroos watch from beside the track
while bright sun washes frost from noon;
they don't move from their warming.

Button daisies watch young wattles
flower among tea trees
she oaks and juvenile eucalypts
where regenerators replicate nature.

Outsiders say our town
spoiled a good sheep paddock.
Now the forest is coming back.

Journeys of the Young

Autumn's chill begins to test the young
A dozen grey fantails swirl though the garden
The birds are small except for two; perhaps the only adults
among start of autumn juveniles.
Weebills zip to drink at the garden's terracotta bird bath.
An eastern spinebill splashes fluttering orange;
silver-eyes and red-browed firetails are brisk and focused.
Stragglers stop to perch before flitting on the journey
of the seasonal flock.

A squabbling crèche of laurel-blotched rosellas
argues its way across the garden
with brief stops on wires or branches
fully immersed in their din.

Below the brow of the hill
in shining black
loitering with dubious intent
a non-breeding flock of little ravens
surveys the slope and valley.

A wedge-tailed eagle with rufous juvenile tint
alights in a eucalypt near the fire trail.
Currawongs and magpies taunt its arrival;
five times their size it seems uncertain.
Ruffled the eagle rests, changes perches
then lifts flying flat
and spirals slowly upward on steady wind
to quarter above the crest of the hill
before gliding from sight.

The young will fly into winter
disperse and be tested
before proven adults rise
in dapper colour and feather
to bob and swirl spring's dance.

Changing Times

Golden wattle that stuns
in early spring freshness
leaves dim hints.

Now in summer what remains
on the gaunt dark bushes
is dried out dull cream.

The flourish is saved
in shining memory and art
and in smitten photos;

while down the road
crimson bottlebrush blooms.

Other Residents

The Move

Finding the house for teenage spread
after years of infant cluster
surprised with wildlife squatters
from when former owners travelled.

Possums lived in the roof
bees inside the brick back wall
in the sunny house
near the nature reserve.
Tradesmen evicted both

but now we watch scouts from a swarm
that hangs in the reserve
hover outside the back door
near a join between brick and wood
that was the first hive's entrance.

Echidna

The thundershower douses the thought
of mowing grass with the electric machine.
Instead we follow the trail to check
on birdlife in the tree-rich reserve.
Raven and rosella fledglings are around
but today sees only sparse currawongs
launching for swoops to earth to feed.
A silent group of young eastern greys
watches from under a tree
while adults lope slowly across the contour.

Then from deep memory with a rolling gait
like a giant spiky beetle, honey quills
with blonde spikes, surfing fashion
nervously ripples an adult echidna
aiming to hide beneath a dead tree.
I had thought they had died out.
Later I learn another has been seen.

Welcome Back

Angels clothed in pure white
with sulphur crowns upon their heads
peer down from high branches
above the grassy bark-strewn bowl.
They visit knowing all seasons
will cherish their antics and bobbing dance.
Shining emblems in this sunshine,
gleaming visions in the shade,
their theatre brings exuberance
to brighten southern scenes.
They hold their court until distant
shrieks bid them rise, with calls
that move the flocks onward
to in time, bring joy again.

The rasping calls herald arrival
this morning before bright day.
We stumble out under ashen skies
and watch the stark white birds
wheel between the tall eucalypts
to land on sparse grass to feed
or perch among orange leaves
soon to desert deciduous branches.
Some rise on powerful wings to glean
fine pickings from what from here, looks
like barren ground near a distant gum.
This host has come from mountain frost
comforts us in the chill.

Tree of Life

Fissures in the granite hill
have channelled rain for growth
and the surge of leaves on eucalypts.
Wattle bloom in the spring heatwave.
Paterson's Curse dies to dark purple.

The tall rangy eucalypt beside the fire trail
hosts a clutch of frogmouths each spring.
Walkers check their progress. We spot the nest
check it with binoculars.
The tawny frogmouth streaked grey
and nondescript sits on eggs;
like a remnant stump or misshapen bulge
with a profile like a headless brooding chicken.
The nest has sparse grass poking
sideways like spokes of a small rimless wheel
on a branch that seems unwise and exposed.
Weeks later two fledglings flatten on a branch
not far from the scant nest
trying to cool in the slight northerly.
They use our Chinese elm as nursery.
Beyond belief their method works.

When the frogmouth family moves on
peewees build their cup-shaped nest
on a small branch of the same trackside tree
an image from childhood.
A black and white tail pokes from the nest.
Egg tending alternates without a break;
as one bird flies in from behind
the sitting bird flies out.

Sentinels

We rarely see you although you are near
but a flurry in the Chinese elm
finds you pointing out noisily
a visiting tawny frogmouth;

next in scrub beside the red clay track
a four-strong non-breeding troupe
jousts with a gang of noisy miners
wings blurring olive-gold in sunlight.

Not here the quiet veranda
sitting with cups of tea to watch
satin bowerbirds fossick in the bushes
as a shiny black male builds a bower.

Here the chain mail plumage
shows you as local security.

The Gang

Stragglers that visit the west of the reserve
are harried by irate magpies
but in the north near tracks
that meet below the lookout

a mob of thirty noisy miners moves
in force to capture a gnarled eucalypt
while berating all in earshot; black masks
yellow beaks glaring above their grey.

Eastern rosellas watch from a distance, bemused
worried about the neighbourhood.

Private Party

Our friend is unsure what it is;
a hen whose chest ripples orange
against her garb of charcoal
but the red head of a sudden male shouts
they are gang-gangs; hard to see
two pairs through different parts of the tree.
We stop only metres away
but they are not concerned with us.

Mostly they screech from down the track
like rusty gates swinging to close.
Today they crunch cones on the monkey puzzle tree
and cover the ground with woody husks.
Their calls are quiet as if exchanging
views on the seeds they eat.
They invite no others to their meal.

Resurrections

The blue-tongue lizard on the verge of living
lies limp and motionless, front arms spread eagled
on the orange paving stones of mid-spring.
In the late afternoon it crawls half a metre
then chills until the next day
before it repeats the attempt to move.
The body is slim with ragged black stripes on white;
thirty centimetres long, on the last of winter's rations.
Next day is warm with bright sunshine
heating the visitor at a faster rate;
then it moves to under a bush to start the hunt
as if it never doubted ignition.

Sunning near a brick wall a week later
behind a spring blast
of surging white and purple daisies
lies another languid blue-tongue
after the almost hibernation of winter.
Shovel headed, fifteen centimetres long
it startles the gardener
who calls me to look
more closely than she wanted
in case it is a *brown snake*.
I pick it up with a handkerchief;
it doesn't seem to mind;
and set it in a sunny spot
distant from the weeding.
When we look back half a minute later
the youngster has gone to cover.

There Are Dragons

Behind a fibro garage in outer Sydney
the bearded dragon would flare its open yellow mouth
holding a territory against the intruder.
The barefoot ten-year-old on the mowed grass
knew the realm and had no fear.

In Canberra a generation later
a thirty-centimetre dragon holds
its yearly ground behind the metal back fence
on pale clay that shows through sparse stubble.
A tall eucalypt nearby is its castle.
Today after spring showers
as a troop of currawongs spreads
among the trees in the reserve to call threats
the lizard stands without open-mouthed concern
arching upwards as if watching
for something important in the distance.

As we climb the rocky trail we spot late
another thin from winter, half a metre long
immobile, soaking sunshine
neck frills down
no will for fighting
legs in running position.
We turn aside crushing tread
then walk on without stopping.
On the way back down, the lizard has gone.
No birds of prey are active
only a plan to live onward.

Cunningham Skink

Moving quickly across the track
on this warmest day of spring
a scuttle, a stop to look
then scuttle again, and again
to a hollow log
disappearing inside.
Copper-coloured, thirty centimetres long
In breeding trim, a lizard shining
as if from tight beaded lines
from head to foot.

In balmy early autumn
towards the top of the hill climb
another Cunningham skink
no longer in breeding display
but black with sunlit turquoise fleck
scurries across the dusty track
towards a jumble of large rocks.
At last we meet
after years of walking these trails.

To the Zone

It fell as the screen door opened;
maybe a striped slug, then with feet
then a ten-centimetre marbled gecko
perhaps the reason for the kookaburra sentry.

I picked it up and it sprinted
along my arm out of sight
clinging to wool, in the mirror.
Perhaps the cold snap lured it

towards the house that seemed warm heaven.
But it is poisoned paradise
from spraying biting insects.
I held the gecko softly, took it outside

to find a plant it liked.
It left for the striped leaf of a cyclamen
in the microclimate near the wall.

Lying with head over the leaf edge
it looked about then skittered
to possibility with less danger.

Meeting a Local

Early in sparse snake summer
I crunch the well-trod track
towards the reserve's lookout.
Marbled clouds screen a dull sun
as across the rubble strewn fire trail
a two-metre dusty brown ribbon
slowly shows its scales and ribbed colour.
Instinct's warning urgently whispers
arc around – keep to living distance.

On the way back down, the snake
is still there, curving through short grass
near where someone strews parrot seed
no doubt as good for rodents.
The eastern brown is flicking its forks of tongue
along the dirt, testing for traces.
It stops as if to signal it is trying
to concentrate on catching its living;
I turn to follow other traces.

The Fledgling

A very light pink galah
slightly smaller than mother
perches beside her on the high wire
demanding to be fed.

Mother ignores the low screeches.
She flies to the ground
leading her offspring to explore
among the grass for ways to feed.

It is mild early summer.
and the fledgling has a good chance.

Sodden

To the north and south rivers rise
flooding towns and stranding the unwary.
Emergency trucks help those trapped.

Here, clouds park above and pour down rain.
treetops on the hill fade into opaque sky.
The roof is leaking; washing hangs near heaters.

In the yard a crèche of rosellas, darkest olive
with only glimpses of belly crimson
graze fallen cotoneaster berries

looking like low-slung herbivores with thick tails.
A group of currawongs drifts over like spectres
and claim a tree for watching.

Smaller birds dissolve into shrubs
to forage another day.

Cool Time

The wall of rain emptied in frenzy
leaving mild grey midwinter.
Brighter crimson draws my eye
to one of three rosellas on the wire
above the kitchen garden.

A mottled hen flies in to perch
then huddles nearby watching.
The nearest cock bird straightens
and strikes a chesty pose.
The next along begins to groom

while the brightest coloured
does not move until a minute later
when he quickly flies away.
The other two leave in the opposite direction
leaving her owning winter wire.

Patches

Through its first cold dry winter
the young grey butcherbird, bedraggled
hunted around the houses near the reserve
snatching enough insects from shrubs
near brick walls heated from within;
purloined some dog food and survived.

In spring the now adult bird moved to the forest
on the nearby hill, smooth-feathered,
reaping from a larger menu.
As it flies through the trees it looks unusual.
When it stops I see patches
dark and light, grey body, brown wings
white face, black head and tail.
I don't spot grey butcherbirds often in the forest
except in active breeding time.

Later another perches in slim profile
on a high wire near tall eucalypts
searching with the stare of a hunter
down its pointed black-tipped beak.
Perhaps it builds strength
or feeds a hen that waits on a stick nest.
Then the week before Christmas
three half-sized black and grey fledglings
sit in line on a low dry branch beside the track.
The oldest watches as I thread my way.

Echoes in the Night

They call through darkness
up the slope among the trees
haunting questions and replies.
They used to roost to snooze the day
in a tree across the fence;
four assorted small brown owls
youngsters, pale and flecked
and adults sporting vertical stripes.
Wide-eyed they watched me watching them.

The neighbours moved and the tree was felled.
I don't see those birds now, but still they sound;
southern boobooks that range wide.
Down south my granddaughter speaks
first phrases from the animal world
'hoo hoo – hoo hoo!'

Remnants

Brown and fluffy stuff of nursery rhymes
a rabbit kitten hops in our back garden
while one next door eats their roses.
We always see a few each spring.

Beside the trail in the nature reserve
one full grown and two half-grown scamper.
Near the top of the hill two more
head for cover.

They are remnants of past plagues
that ate the lives of farmers.
A little eagle watches from an apple box eucalypt.

Teaching

From the dusty track this late spring twilight
off to the side, a hare is slowly hopping
among low bush and long grass.
It looks distracted and doesn't see
us walking from upwind;

odd, as mostly hares bound off
along the contour, white-pipped ears erect.
This one is camouflage grey, large-eyed
ears standing proud. Then, slowly it crouches
as ears flatten onto the back and it disappears.

The act looks conscious
as if a lesson
to young hiding there from harm.

Juliet Who Survived the Fox

When the raid came there were ten
ider brown hens, barely one year old.
The fox got at them by digging under wire

into the quaint henhouse yard. Six were killed;
there was gore but three were gone, stashed.
One was injured and later died.

Later, two with stress were given
to neighbours over the road. During the carnage
Juliet was visiting next door.

That was two years ago. Now at night
she sleeps in a safe tree, clear
of the haunted hen house.

Today she wanders in the back door
to peck the floor. She will be lifted
and carried out by the boy, as ever.

On a Branch

A finely tiger-coloured sporran of bees
with over a thousand animal souls
a swarm in the surge of spring
hangs on a small gum tree in the reserve.
Workers fly off and back drowsy with gorged honey
that scents the air for twenty metres around.
Within, the old queen waits on news of her next home.
Her former hive is close in the giant eucalypt
with the glinting stream of wings and the daughter queen.

I cared for hives as a teenager;
a rural cotton-clad rent collector with gauze mask
bearing an iron hive tool and distracting smoke.
Under one hive a copperhead, cousin of the cobra briefly kept warm.
Bee stings were less painful than falls and scrapes in paddocks
or punishments for young misdemeanours.
I hot-knifed full combs and spun out sweetness
while bees worked for the common good.

Saving the Future

Weeks of heavy storms and showers from cyclones
sent their moisture from the north
yet branches and trunks still have drought-tortured forms
along the now refreshed forest trail
where leaves are lush bulging green.

Wattles strengthen to bloom.
Eucalypts shed bark for stripes on trunks
and to show off insect-designed tattoos.
Mistletoe flowers white in the upper canopy
while atop the drought-straggled branches
of the blackthorn forest understorey

a field of bunches of orange seed pod
prepares to make deposits for the future.

She Oak Bloom

She seems the strong one, always here
not looking like she changes much
while eucalypts around drop limbs in stress
or die back branches in dry spells.
If steady rains bring rot
to thick-barked trees nearby

her tough bark shell
endures and holds together.
When frost labours breath
and snow caps the hills
her long fingered fronds maintain
firm sweeps beside the track.

Now in kinder time
with calming rain and lengthening days
she at last allows herself a fling
short orange blossoms lighten her skirt.

Winter Welcome

They call you wanderer
but you are *hardenbergia*
and on this bleak afternoon

when no bird sings
beside the stone-strewn fire trail
you lift your pointed leaves

your glowing violet flowers
from tangled reclining vines
to greet the fertile months.

Visitors

Yellow-tailed Black Cockatoos

swirl on the winter southerly bluster
above a Canberra suburb
that has not seen them this year.
Good spring breeding has sent a dense flock.

Soon rasping debate rages
from dark forms barely visible in treetops.
Elsewhere they crack pine cones for seeds
here they forage in eucalypt canopy.

The shortest day was two past
and today is only minutes longer
but some are already in courtly mode.
A pair chatters excitedly.
Two others check a hollow
while another watches from a nearby tree.

Noisy argument within the flock subsides
as it swarms within rowdy shrieks
that hold a bond and set direction.
With measured calls they calm
and with loping wing beats move on.

The Return

Eagles appeared suddenly on the hill
yesterday flying still in the wind
two sets of black wings held fingers spread
like on an ancient shield.
Today they perch on strong talons, crooked beaks
taunted by miniature magpies.

Decades back on a family trip
we saw eagles strung dead
wing tip to wing tip on miles of barbed fences.
Sheep grazed the dry grass behind.
Deaths for crimes against rural livelihood
were later eclipsed by DDT.

For years a reclusive pair of survivors
has worked the roads from Mugga Ridge to the south.
Each year they send their young to fly
until this season with good rains for growth and
food for extra chicks
returns wedge-taileds to Red Hill.

After Dry Years

A small flock of king parrots
perches in a tall gum tree
beside the track in the reserve.
Three are female, four are male
brilliant in red and green.

Perhaps because of this kinder year
a cock bird explores a hollow
from interest or instinct.

Mild times see flocks swell
to spread their ranges
into surprised forests.

Rarely

On the first short sleeve day of spring
a rare call turns my head
towards the branches of the Chinese elm
now sprouting early mint green leaves.

A hoarse almost croaky chirp repeats
to sound the trees nearby for a friend.
Oddly it is only in this tree
I glimpse the migrant satin flycatcher.

It perches less than sparrow small with black head
formally plumed in white and black.
Leaden flycatchers sometimes visit dressed in grey
but mostly it is their satin cousins
calling down the years.

Rain Chasers

They are back after rainier seasons
crimson and black, the hens almost pink
thornbill small, moving through
the eucalypt canopy on the hill
as the core of an unusual mixed flock
with eastern spinebills, grey fantails
some thornbills and eastern warblers.

It has been eight years since I noted
crimson chats like these in the field notebook
before the long dry set in
but at the same time of year.
The nomads have followed the rain back.
Wattle has begun to bloom.
It is Ngunnawal First Spring.
I hope they stay to breed.

Among the Leaves

The first to come peers without malice
from the wires towards the forest branches
in the nearby slope. That afternoon we watch

both pallid cuckoos, grey on grey with rounded heads
prison stripes on their tails, fly wings-spread
half gliding above the canopy

into a slow west wind, searching downward
for the nest to con with their egg and the large chick
that will eject other nestlings for their feeds.

The time of crime passes into heat
and the cuckoos and their young move on
in nature's daunting tolerance.

Returning to the Hollow

As if a starting gun has been fired
magpies sprint from all directions
disrupting the peace of the hill.
There must be twenty from nearby territories
flapping black and white wings
with focused aim that forms a flying cone
to harass the visitor
a light nankeen-coloured kestrel
midsize and young, likely a female
that speeds its glide from grassland to forest
to be hidden among the trees.

Days are lengthening; kestrels have nested here
in the grey hollow of a gum tree near the track.
Is the instinctive explosion of magpies
out of fear of something now unaccustomed
or to drive away a potential neighbour
that might glean the same food
or threaten their young?

At the end of spring's first month
frosts are gone as days lengthen and warm;
showers green the forest.
The kestrel returns after absence
to visit every day or two then stay
perched on an upper branch of a tall eucalypt
fifty metres from another ancient yellow box
with dead grey limbs, broken and hollow.
She watches for movement and gazes at one hollow.

After a week she darts there to nest.
She starts to house clean and prepare
then stands at the opening watching
outward and seemingly inward
at something developing there.

The pair are hyper wary
attempting invisibility through speed
and mostly succeeding so all that is in view
is a fast disappearing speedster
seventy metres from the nest hollow.

Over months their presence is constant;
indian myna sentries the giveaway
as they wait to scrounge the feeding scraps.
Currawongs terrorise the small male kestrel
and after that he is rarely seen near the tree;
the hen brings baby snakes and other prey
but looks steadily more worn

Today at last from a tall sparse eucalypt
along the grass-rimmed trail near the nursery tree
three strong fledglings watch.

Robins

What lands near me is new
the colours understated
but the shape says robin.
Small brown birds are hard to pick
as they flit through the forest.
Watchers need a clearer look
than the one second
that calls out mumbled confusion.
My luck – a colourful mate appears
giving a pair to match with the book:
rose robins wintering from colder hills.

Another comes this time of year
as one of the changing colours of autumn
a mountain volunteer for mixed flocks;
impossible to ignore – like a stop sign
with a beaming scarlet breast
bright white above the beak
and on wings that flash
as he flits between trees and shrubs.
The robin seems to want not to intrude
as he perches in the tree that I walk past
or on a wire near the fire trail
as I limbo into the reserve.
His mate is less brightly coloured
I see her mostly from a distance.

On the Move

Migrating birds cheep among the branches
calling back and forth in the early autumn mixed flock
in the Namadgi Reserve in Tidbinbilla.

A ranger says that honeyeaters have been moving
through for the last two weeks out of cold ranges
towards the warmer plains.

A flitting group dips and drinks clear creek water;
a white-naped honeyeater darts back to foliage
as a restless flycatcher grooms, crisp white against black.

A call lifts the mostly hidden flock to move on.
A week later fifty kilometres west
on the nature corridor on our hill

a golden whistler pipes plaintively to his flock
as if searching for something to fuel the journey.
Bright shining feathers beneath a white mask
he restlessly hops from branch to branch.

From the Storm

Spring rain then belting hail
broke branches and half-filled buckets
before we walked the nature corridor.

A nervous sacred kingfisher flits.
Further on calls echo from a large eucalypt
but we can't see the caller in the crush of leaves.

Next day I bring binoculars and spy
the white and black flecked underside
of the bird that flies to a high branch.

I see the olive sunlit wings
the long orange beak
of the olive-backed oriole, the first in three years.

A week later it still calls in hope.

Long Distance Little Eagle

After they tagged her, she flew north
to winter near Charters Towers then returned.
Now she glides on easterly sea breezes above Red Hill
in heatwave dusk.
In weather like this Canberra burned.

The eagle beak is etched against the sky
as her mate rises from a large tree downslope.
He wintered in Melbourne City.
Harassed by magpies he joins to quarter
scanning for rabbits unusually absent.

Sitting high into the rising wind
above the trig point
she is a steady still miniature
until with smooth descent
angled and almost all glide
without wing movement
she lands on the branch of the brittle gum.

Half-light at dusk shows the eagle brown with fingered wing tips
almost twice as big as a magpie, bigger than a kestrel
smaller than wedge-taileds. She rises above the high ridge
to land in a tree before the kangaroo-killing road.
Next morning she is back in a fire-painted eucalypt
a bloodied rabbit carcass in her grasp
guarding a home coming gift from the hill.

After an absent month nesting on Black Mountain
irate currawongs berate her;
perched, feathers seem ragged
perhaps from harried maternity
a growing chick in the nest.
Rising again into the wind
the white bars on underwings
give the sign for little eagle.

Feathers become smooth again
as the notch in flights on one wing
confirms she is the Traveller.
Last season's fledgling has flown to Adelaide.

Painted Ladies

Walking a kangaroo contour track
through thick forest beside the fire trail
I hear small birds but see few in denser foliage
from drought breaking rain.
Ahead and beside me a cloud of butterflies
rises in mesmerising sidestepping flight.
They are painted ladies, fresh orange and black
resting down slope from a field of yellow daisies
that their young feed on, thick this year
between white flowering shrubs
wattles, tea trees and she oaks
under the yellow box eucalypt canopy.
Each summer painted ladies fly hundreds of kilometres
to breed on this hill. With brown field argus and others
they have hung on for this kinder summer.

Pasture Day Moth

After another freezing night
midwinter caterpillars
with orange heads, black fur, yellow tail spots
emerged four centimetres long
from circular holes to burrows
to graze in mid-afternoon.
They scattered thinly near the dusty track
at the foot of the hill climb.
Birds must not like their taste
because each day they reappeared
leaving only the odd dead one
perhaps from starving with little vegetation.

Sometimes they manage to damage crops
as they feed for orange and cream flight
and their breeding surge.
Mostly they are minor pests
living quiet but colourful lives.

Something New

On a soggy summer afternoon an unusual
green parrot flies straight to a small nest hollow
gnawed around the east-facing opening
ten metres high on the grey and white streaked trunk
of a brittle gum near the top of the hill climb.
A second bird follows quickly;
only green can be seen except
for a flash of colours
when it disappears like the first;
leaving a memory of fifteen seconds of flights.

They are rainbow lorikeets from the east
bushfire refugees from Black Summer
that fled from coastal gum forests to Canberra
to nest in this eucalypt in the reserve
managing to raise chicks.

Wood Ducks

An unusual clutch a ducklings
parades along the suburban street;
the duck, flecked; the drake, smooth grey;
ducklings with clouded yellow down

hatched in a hollow high in a tree
a blended family with some absent mothers
who found a rare nest to add their eggs
and swell the brood.

In mid-spring the parents lead twelve ducklings
searching for water that is nowhere close.
Sometimes these parades go a kilometre
across busy roads to reach a pond.

Ducklings cling to life
through the rough start
to grow into their promise.

Scarce

Unearthly dog like howling
sounds through the eucalypt hill
as I trudge the dusty track at dusk.

The cry has rung out for days
so I wind my way
up the slope to where I hear

the white-faced, yellow-eyed hawk owl
bigger and paler than a boobook
perched on a bare branch.

Some say it sounds like a woman screaming;
it doesn't sound like a fox.
It is the scarce night hunter

the soulful barking owl.

Leaving the Nest

The late day heat is soothed by easterly winds
as we trudge towards the haloed hill crest.
There a young grey falcon hangs still in air
then sweeps a halting curve to land
on the branch of an apple box eucalypt.

There is no drop onto prey
that an old hawk might have found.
The large youngster has successfully fledged
thick feathers nourished by constant parents
to appear as rare visitor.

At an age when dull-coloured magpies
still fed by parents
learn to fossick on the forest floor
the falcon has travelled to this new territory
to risk its way alone.

Family Feud

Dim shapes are sparring
dark dancers against the sky
lunging and gliding apart.
Shapes and sizes seem the same.
We climb the hill above the treeline
to find a clearer view.

The squabblers finally part to show
falcon underwings of their type;
one the almost white of the kestrel
the other the dark and light of the hobby
a little falcon we have not seen here before.
They are alike except in close view.
These strangers probe in angry suspicion
look like a family fight.

Skirmish

As we walk beneath late day cloud cover
a heat-bedraggled kestrel hen watches
from a rot-carved grotto
high in a battered eucalypt

a file of choughs that caravans
across a magpie family's territory
fixedly feeding on what is close.
With dogged intent, the group

like a procession of black-robed monks
for good reason, walking briskly.
Amid magpie battle calls they face attack
their group swelled by good breeding months.

Repulsing lunges with snappy defence
they cluster, backs arched, tails and wings fanned
showing white feathers underwing
to seem more imposing, while they edge to safety.

Choughs are rarely seen here;
they look to be just walking through.

Forest Grounding

The Climb

Five months after the gift
of a bovine heart valve
my body does not feel normal.

Short walks are tough
but I attempt at last
the long-favoured hill climb.

My absence seems to draw rebuke;
each step is cautious
pausing to sense reaction

as the trail winds upwards
under clouds that hide the sun
until at last from veins and sinews

deep and surface mind
joy surges as the body remembers.
This hill remains my friend.

Naming Seasons

From the Antarctic to the high tropics
seasons are clerically decreed
the earth squeezed into four sizes.

Here blossoms blast in midwinter;
kookaburras cackle territory;
a galah gnaws the mouth of last year's nest hollow.

First People quietly ignore the folly
and keep on calling many more seasons
when and how they come.

A Different Path

In a forest I thought well known
I found a different path that day
through where undergrowth seemed too thick
to let a traveller through.

Behind a wall of saplings
I found a clearing
that held the start of a wide track
worn enough to think it had lasted.

The track thinned and split into choices
through straggling clinging branches
rejoined for a hard climb
then lead to wide vistas

at a place I am content to be.

Along the Track

Two nankeen kestrels with honey wings
over pale bodies, hunt
through a rare long stay, roosting together
until only one is seen. The smaller bird
likely the younger, still seizes prey and returns
to a quiet spot among large trees.
I think there is a nest – doubtless in a hollow.

It seems too soon when the second bird
perches ruffled and alone as if she has stopped waiting
for eggs to hatch or has no young to feed.
Four currawongs harass her
from perches a metre away, below and above
and at the side. They dart in snapping
without seeming to do much damage.

Later she perches at the top
of a gnarled grey almost leafless eucalypt.
It looks a time of disappointment;
perhaps next season will be kinder.
The currawongs move to capture
the bird bath in the backyard, and the tree
near the steps as a nursery.
Then in the reserve I see with surprise
the two kestrels glide to a sparse treetop
manoeuvre almost joyfully, then separate.
Close above me, near a grey hollow
their fledgling, dull-coloured and short-tailed
still days from flying, perches and silently
watches as I navigate my trail.

Two years after Black Summer

towns rise again but struggle
wildlife slowly returns

as beside a country highway
a long green padded wall
of fresh eucalypt leaves
grows from short branches
out of blackened trunks
filling out the shape of each tree
below bare burnt upper branches.
Rare trees regrow at their height.

Along from the green wall
in an unburnt stretch recent rain
has grown tall grasses;
a pine plantation caught by fire
stands black and lifeless

but a sparse eucalypt forest sports
new growth on thick charred limbs
before a dense rise of native saplings.

Recharge

Soft rain gifts me the trail
through the forest to the hill
past eucalypts colouring mottled trunks yellow.
Greener foliage is emerging
but some leather leaves endure.

Magpies barely pause as I pass.
Kangaroos watch with little curiosity.
A cockatoo screeches overhead.
In the west through clouds
the last sunglow shows patches of blue sky.

At the top of the hill the breeze strokes my face.

Listening

We travelled far to see the clear skies
the looming trees that try to claim it;
to hear the silence and sense
what it holds; to find fresh nature.

In the city the skies are crowded
with thrusting angles; streets are filled
by noise and need; the smooth voices
of greed hold hope for gain
as they reign in turn.

On the hill the eucalypts blanket
the living space where kangaroos
birds and insects cycle from birth
to birth again, and we hear once more
silence and wild calls on the breeze.

www.ingramcontent.com/pod-product-compliance
Lightning Source LLC
Chambersburg PA
CBHW071023080526
44587CB00015B/2476